30 WAYS TO KILL DEPRESSION

By

HIMANSHU DEORI

HIMANSHU DEORI

30 WAYS TO KILL DEPRESSION

HIMANSHU DEORI

30 WAYS TO KILL DEPRESSION

Dedicated to all youths

HIMANSHU DEORI

30 WAYS TO KILL DEPRESSION

STATISTIC REPORT ON DEPRESSION:

Depression is a significant global health concern, affecting hundreds of millions of individuals worldwide. According to the World Health Organization (WHO), as of 2015, over 300 million people globally were estimated to suffer from depression, accounting for approximately 4.3% of the world's population.

iris.who.int

In India, the prevalence of depression is also notable. The National Mental Health Survey 2015-16 revealed that nearly 15% of Indian adults require active intervention for one or more mental health issues, with one in 20 Indians suffering from depression.

who.int

Focusing on the youth demographic, a UNICEF report highlighted that among Indians aged 15 to 24, one in seven often feels depressed or has little interest in doing things. This data underscores the mental health challenges faced by young individuals in the country.

economictimes.indiatimes.com

It's important to note that these statistics may have evolved since the time of these reports, especially considering the global events and societal changes that have occurred in recent years. Continuous monitoring and updated studies are essential to understand the current landscape of mental health both globally and within specific populations.

HIMANSHU DEORI

30 WAYS TO KILL DEPRESSION

HIMANSHU DEORI

30 WAYS TO KILL DEPRESSION

Acknowledgment

This book would not have been possible without the unwavering support, encouragement, and inspiration from many people who have touched my life. To my family and friends, thank you for being my rock during difficult times and for reminding me of the beauty and strength in connection. To the countless individuals who shared their stories of resilience and healing, your courage has been my greatest source of motivation.

A heartfelt thank you to mental health professionals, researchers, and advocates around the world, whose work continues to illuminate paths to recovery and hope. Lastly, to you, the reader—thank you for taking this brave step toward healing and transformation. This book is dedicated to everyone striving to overcome the darkness and embrace the light. Together, we are stronger.

HIMANSHU DEORI

30 WAYS TO KILL DEPRESSION

Introduction

Depression can feel like an overwhelming, all-consuming shadow that clouds your thoughts, drains your energy, and makes joy seem out of reach. But the truth is, depression is not invincible. With the right tools, mindset, and strategies, you can take meaningful steps toward healing and reclaiming your life. This book presents 30 actionable ways to combat depression, providing you with a comprehensive toolkit to break free from its grip. Whether you're looking for small, manageable changes or larger transformative practices, this book offers something for everyone. Let's embark on this journey together and uncover the possibilities for hope and recovery.

Depression can affect anyone at any stage of life, and it doesn't discriminate based on age, gender, or background. It can stem from a range of factors, including life stressors, traumatic experiences, genetic predispositions, or imbalances in brain

HIMANSHU DEORI

30 WAYS TO KILL DEPRESSION

chemistry. The key to overcoming it is recognizing that you have the power to change your circumstances—even if the steps feel small at first. This book is divided into practical sections, addressing everything from physical self-care to emotional growth, cognitive tools, and long-term strategies to keep depression at bay. Every journey begins with a single step. Start yours today.

HIMANSHU DEORI

30 WAYS TO KILL DEPRESSION

AUTHOR'S NOTE:

Dear Readers,

I have personally overcome depression, a traumatic experience that has become increasingly prevalent among the younger generation in recent years. While I don't claim to know the root cause of this issue, my extensive research and personal experience have led me to conclude that depression can be overcome by following a series of steps.

Unfortunately, depression has claimed many lives, making it a pressing concern. Through my observations and research, I have come to realize that depression is a persistent issue, caused by various factors, and cannot be eliminated entirely. However, most people struggle to cope with it or don't know the necessary steps to take when

HIMANSHU DEORI

30 WAYS TO KILL DEPRESSION

severely depressed. This is why I believe I have found an effective solution.

To achieve mental and physical well-being and overcome depression, I have summarized 30 practical steps in this book. I genuinely hope that this book will resonate with and assist young people who are struggling with depression. The sole purpose of this book is to provide support and guidance to those affected by depression.

HIMANSHU DEORI

30 WAYS TO KILL DEPRESSION

Part 1: Building the Foundations of Healing

1. **Acknowledge Your Feelings**

   Accept that it's okay to feel how you're feeling. Denying your emotions only makes them more overwhelming. Sometimes, simply naming what you're experiencing can bring clarity and relief.

HIMANSHU DEORI

30 WAYS TO KILL DEPRESSION

HIMANSHU DEORI

30 WAYS TO KILL DEPRESSION

2. Seek Professional Help

A therapist, counselor, or psychiatrist can provide guidance and tools tailored to your situation. Therapy offers a safe space to explore your thoughts and feelings without judgment. Medication, when recommended, can also play a crucial role in balancing brain chemistry.

30 WAYS TO KILL DEPRESSION

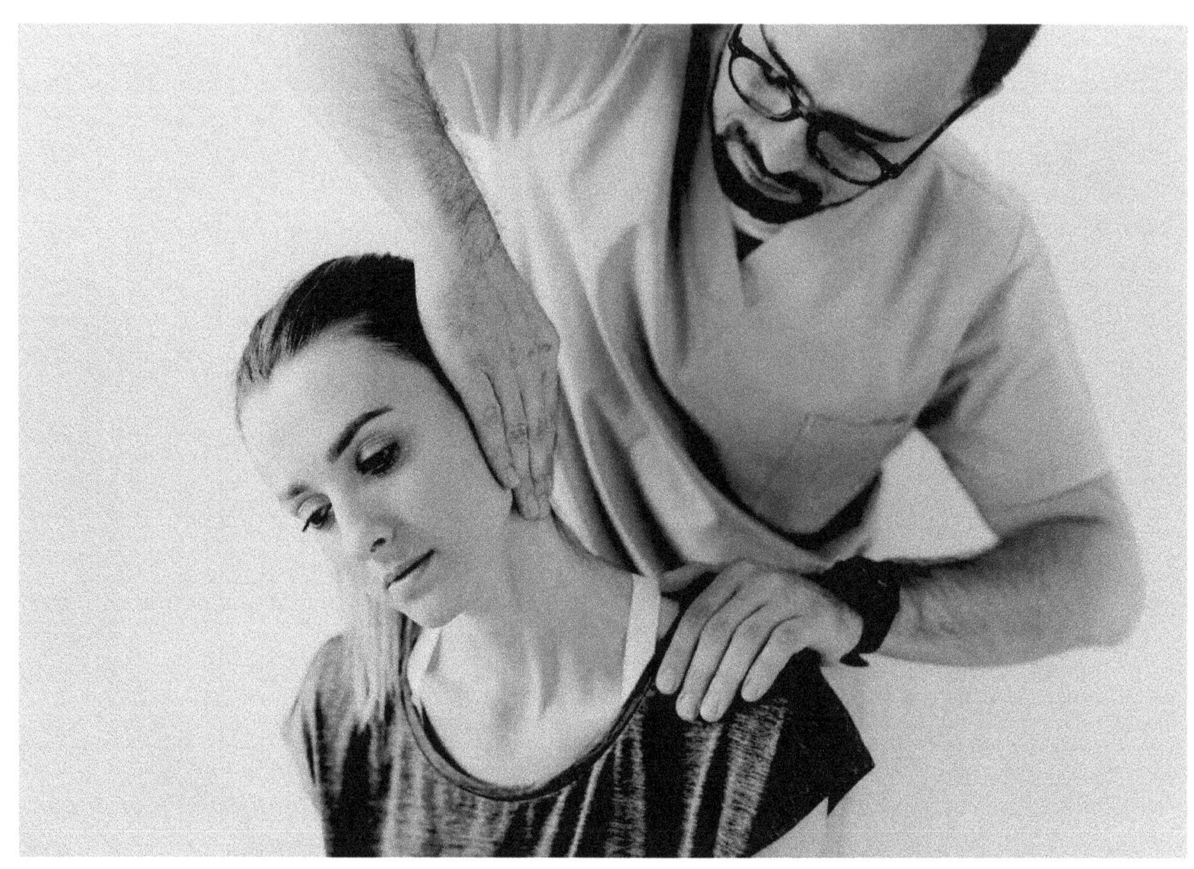

HIMANSHU DEORI

30 WAYS TO KILL DEPRESSION

3. **Educate Yourself About Depression**
   Understanding the biological, psychological, and social aspects of depression can demystify your experience. Learning about depression helps you see that it's a medical condition, not a personal failing. Books, articles, and reputable online resources can be valuable tools.

HIMANSHU DEORI

30 WAYS TO KILL DEPRESSION

HIMANSHU DEORI

30 WAYS TO KILL DEPRESSION

4. Create a Support System

Surround yourself with people who care about you and understand your struggles. Reach out to trusted friends or family members, and don't hesitate to lean on them for support during tough times. Connection is one of the antidotes to isolation.

HIMANSHU DEORI

30 WAYS TO KILL DEPRESSION

HIMANSHU DEORI

30 WAYS TO KILL DEPRESSION

5. **Set Small, Achievable Goals**

   Start with simple tasks, like getting out of bed or making your bed, to build momentum. Small victories can create a sense of accomplishment and provide a foundation for tackling larger challenges over time.

HIMANSHU DEORI

30 WAYS TO KILL DEPRESSION

GOAL SETTING

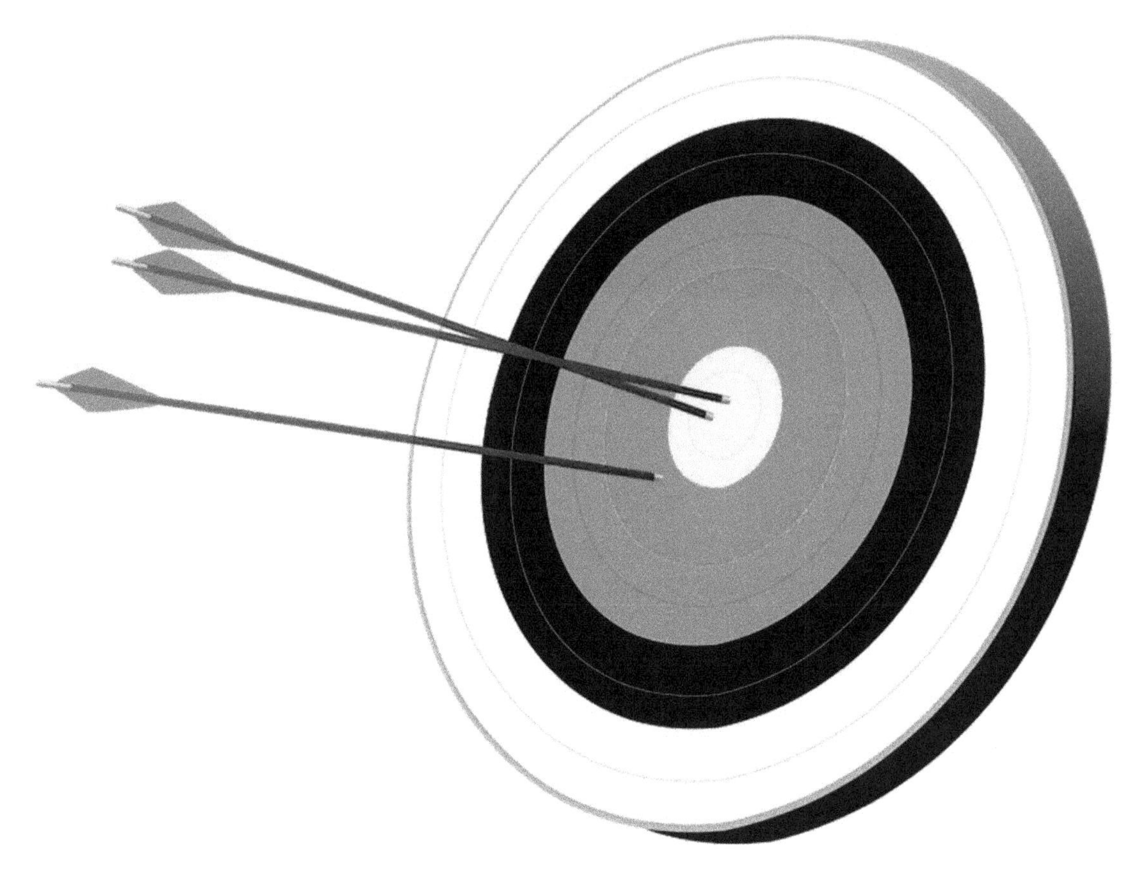

HIMANSHU DEORI

30 WAYS TO KILL DEPRESSION

6. Establish a Routine

Structure provides stability and can help you regain a sense of normalcy. A predictable routine can act as an anchor, especially during periods of emotional turbulence. Even creating a basic daily schedule can make a difference.

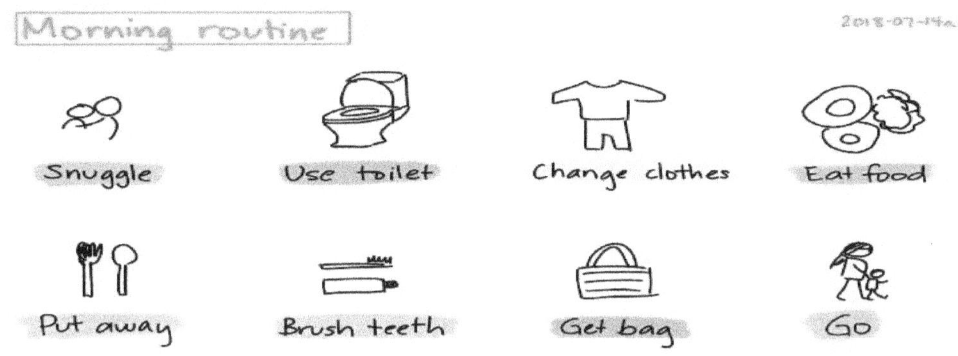

HIMANSHU DEORI

30 WAYS TO KILL DEPRESSION

HIMANSHU DEORI

30 WAYS TO KILL DEPRESSION

7. **Practice Gratitude**

   Write down three things you're grateful for each day, no matter how small. Gratitude shifts your focus away from negativity and helps you recognize the positive aspects of your life, even during difficult times.

HIMANSHU DEORI

30 WAYS TO KILL DEPRESSION

8. Limit Stressful Triggers

Identify and reduce exposure to people, places,

HIMANSHU DEORI

30 WAYS TO KILL DEPRESSION

or situations that exacerbate your depression. Creating boundaries and saying no to unnecessary stressors can safeguard your mental health.

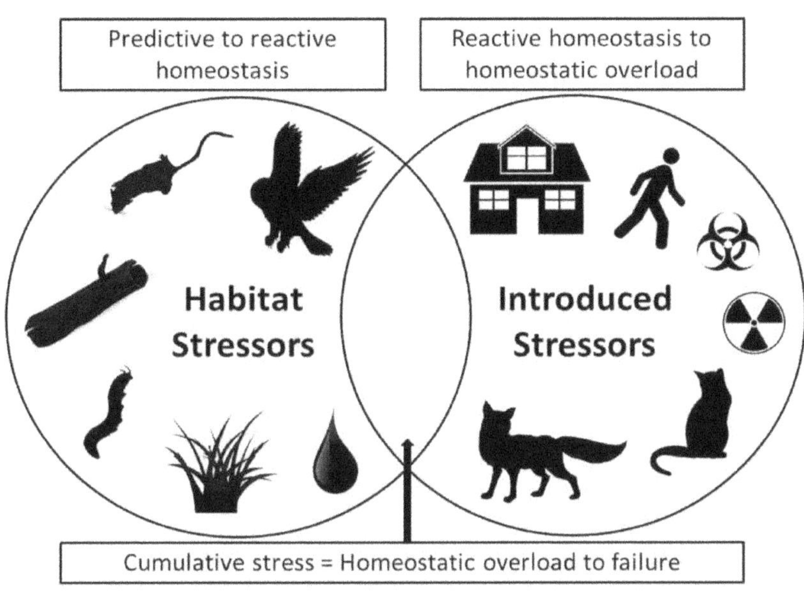

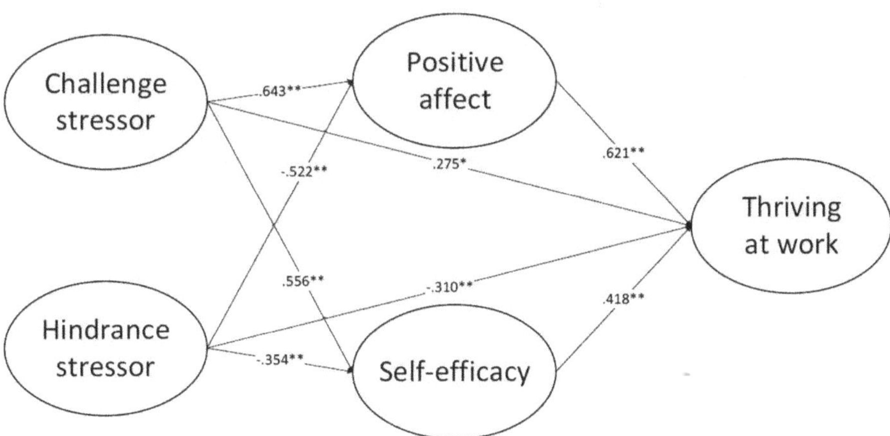

9. Identify Negative Thought Patterns

Challenge and replace thoughts like "I'm a

HIMANSHU DEORI

30 WAYS TO KILL DEPRESSION

failure" with more balanced perspectives. Cognitive-behavioral techniques can help you break free from the cycle of negativity and self-criticism.

10.   **Embrace Imperfection**

Recognize that no one is perfect, and that's okay. Strive for progress, not perfection. Accepting your imperfections can free you from unrealistic expectations and unnecessary

30 WAYS TO KILL DEPRESSION

pressure.

HIMANSHU DEORI

30 WAYS TO KILL DEPRESSION

Part 2: Physical Steps to Combat Depression

11.   Exercise Regularly

Physical activity boosts endorphins and reduces stress hormones. Start small with activities like walking, stretching, or dancing, and gradually build up to more intense workouts if you're able.

HIMANSHU DEORI

30 WAYS TO KILL DEPRESSION

HIMANSHU DEORI

30 WAYS TO KILL DEPRESSION

12. **Practice Deep Breathing**

Controlled breathing can calm your mind and reduce anxiety. Techniques like diaphragmatic breathing or the 4-7-8 method can help you feel more grounded and present.

HIMANSHU DEORI

30 WAYS TO KILL DEPRESSION

HIMANSHU DEORI

30 WAYS TO KILL DEPRESSION

13.   Improve Your Sleep Hygiene

Stick to a consistent sleep schedule and create a restful bedtime routine. Avoid screens an hour before bed, keep your bedroom dark and quiet, and consider relaxation techniques to prepare your mind for sleep.

HIMANSHU DEORI

30 WAYS TO KILL DEPRESSION

SLEEP HYGIENE

14. **Eat a Balanced Diet**
     Nutrient-rich foods can improve your brain

HIMANSHU DEORI

30 WAYS TO KILL DEPRESSION

health and mood. Focus on whole foods like fruits, vegetables, lean proteins, and whole grains while limiting processed and sugary items.

HIMANSHU DEORI

30 WAYS TO KILL DEPRESSION

HIMANSHU DEORI

30 WAYS TO KILL DEPRESSION

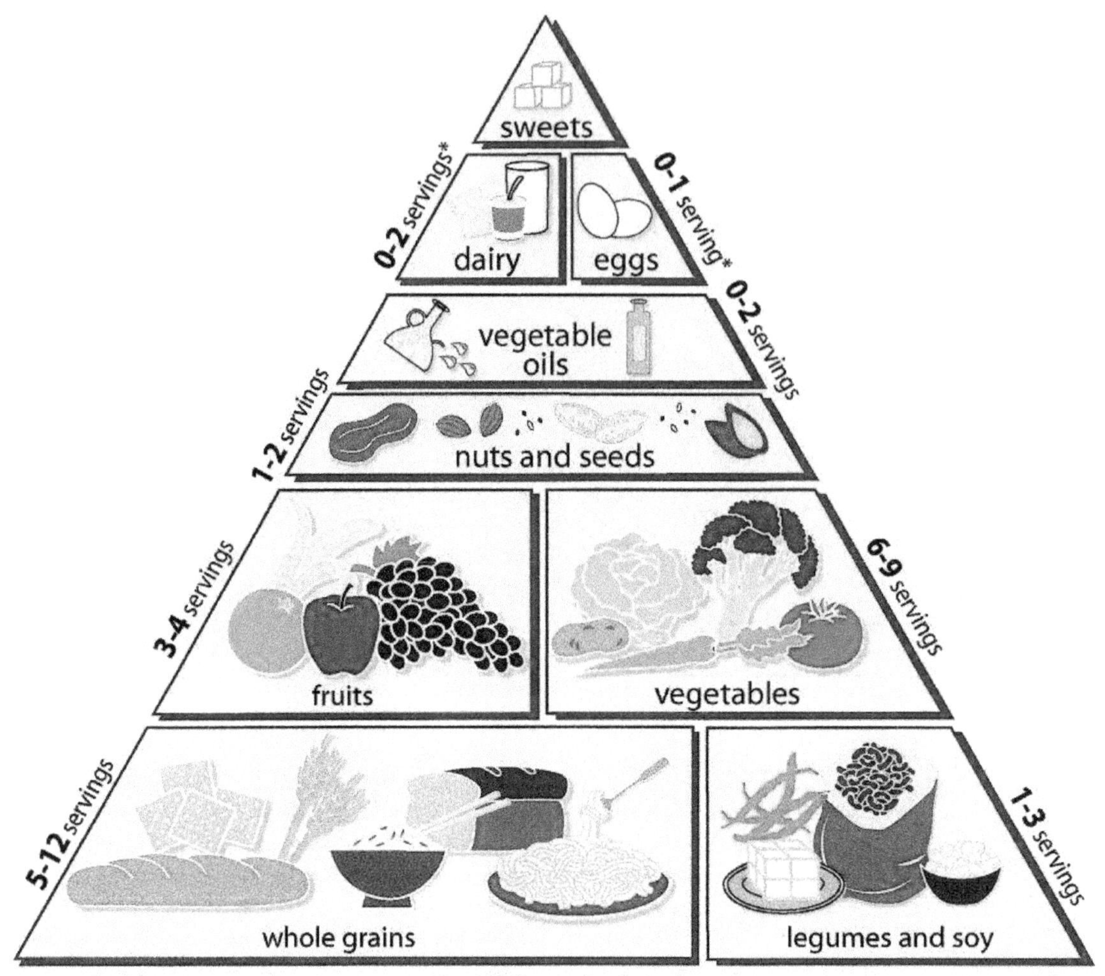

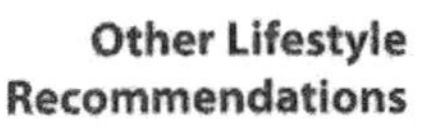

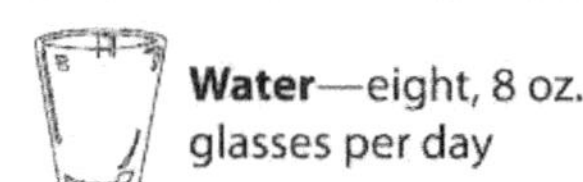

15.   Stay Hydrated

Dehydration can affect your mood and energy levels. Aim to drink enough water throughout the day to keep your body functioning optimally.

HIMANSHU DEORI

30 WAYS TO KILL DEPRESSION

HIMANSHU DEORI

30 WAYS TO KILL DEPRESSION

16. **Take Walks in Nature**

Spending time outdoors can help you feel connected and grounded. Natural settings like parks, forests, or beaches can soothe your mind and provide a sense of peace.

30 WAYS TO KILL DEPRESSION

HIMANSHU DEORI

30 WAYS TO KILL DEPRESSION

HIMANSHU DEORI

30 WAYS TO KILL DEPRESSION

17. Reduce Caffeine Intake

Too much caffeine can increase anxiety and disrupt sleep. Consider switching to decaffeinated options or herbal teas, especially in the afternoon and evening.

HIMANSHU DEORI

30 WAYS TO KILL DEPRESSION

HIMANSHU DEORI

30 WAYS TO KILL DEPRESSION

18.   **Try Yoga**

Yoga combines physical movement with mindfulness to promote relaxation. Even a short session can leave you feeling calmer and more centered.

HIMANSHU DEORI

30 WAYS TO KILL DEPRESSION

HIMANSHU DEORI

30 WAYS TO KILL DEPRESSION

19.   Use Aromatherapy

Scents like lavender and chamomile can have

30 WAYS TO KILL DEPRESSION

calming effects. Consider using essential oils, candles, or diffusers to create a soothing atmosphere.

HIMANSHU DEORI

30 WAYS TO KILL DEPRESSION

20. **Take Breaks from Technology**

Excessive screen time can contribute to feelings of isolation and overwhelm. Set boundaries around your phone, social media, and other devices to give your mind a break.

HIMANSHU DEORI

30 WAYS TO KILL DEPRESSION

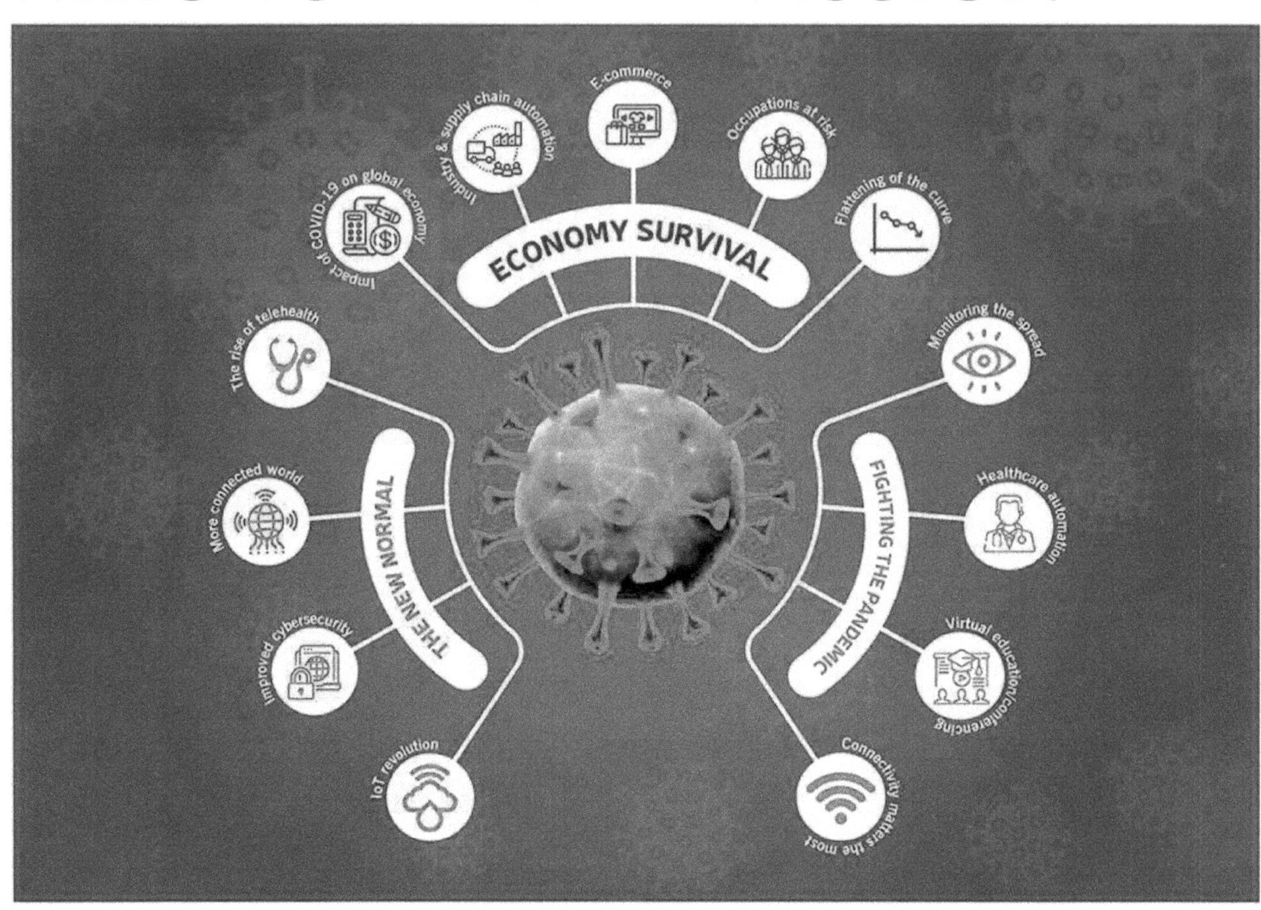

HIMANSHU DEORI

30 WAYS TO KILL DEPRESSION

Part 3: Mindset Shifts and Cognitive Tools

21.   **Practice Mindfulness**

Stay present and focus on the here and now. Techniques like meditation, grounding exercises, or mindful observation can help you let go of past regrets and future worries.

30 WAYS TO KILL DEPRESSION

22.   **Reframe Challenges**

View obstacles as opportunities for growth. A shift in perspective can transform difficulties into valuable learning experiences.

HIMANSHU DEORI

30 WAYS TO KILL DEPRESSION

HIMANSHU DEORI

30 WAYS TO KILL DEPRESSION

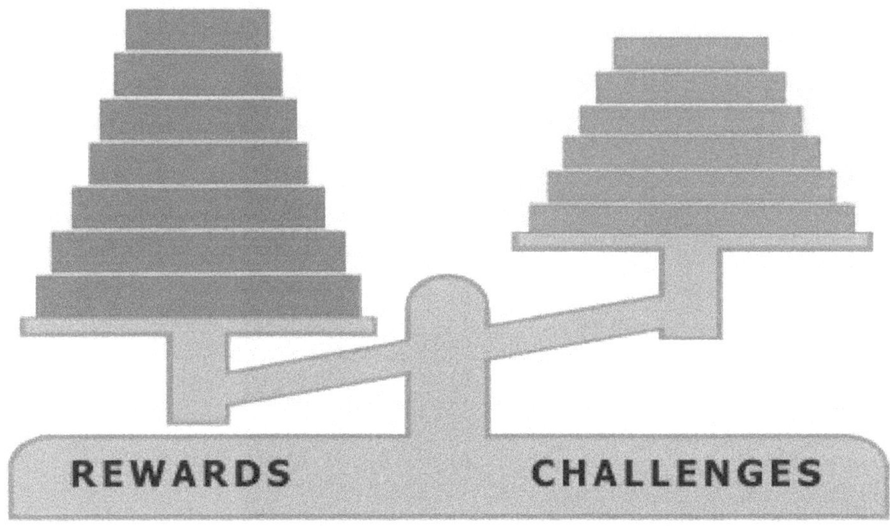

23.   **Write in a Journal**

Expressing your thoughts on paper can provide clarity and relief. Journaling is a safe space to vent, reflect, and explore your emotions without fear of judgment.

HIMANSHU DEORI

30 WAYS TO KILL DEPRESSION

HIMANSHU DEORI

30 WAYS TO KILL DEPRESSION

Challenge Catastrophic Thinking

Replace "What if everything goes wrong?" with "What if everything goes right?" This simple shift can open up new possibilities and reduce unnecessary fear.

24. **Visualize Success**

Imagine yourself overcoming challenges and

30 WAYS TO KILL DEPRESSION

achieving your goals. Visualization can inspire motivation and increase your confidence in taking action.

HIMANSHU DEORI

30 WAYS TO KILL DEPRESSION

HIMANSHU DEORI

30 WAYS TO KILL DEPRESSION

25. Use Positive Affirmations

Repeat affirmations like "I am worthy of happiness" daily. Positive self-talk can help rewire your brain and boost self-esteem over time.

30 WAYS TO KILL DEPRESSION

HIMANSHU DEORI

30 WAYS TO KILL DEPRESSION

26. **Focus on What You Can Control**
Let go of things beyond your influence.
Concentrating on what you can change
empowers you to take effective action.

HIMANSHU DEORI

30 WAYS TO KILL DEPRESSION

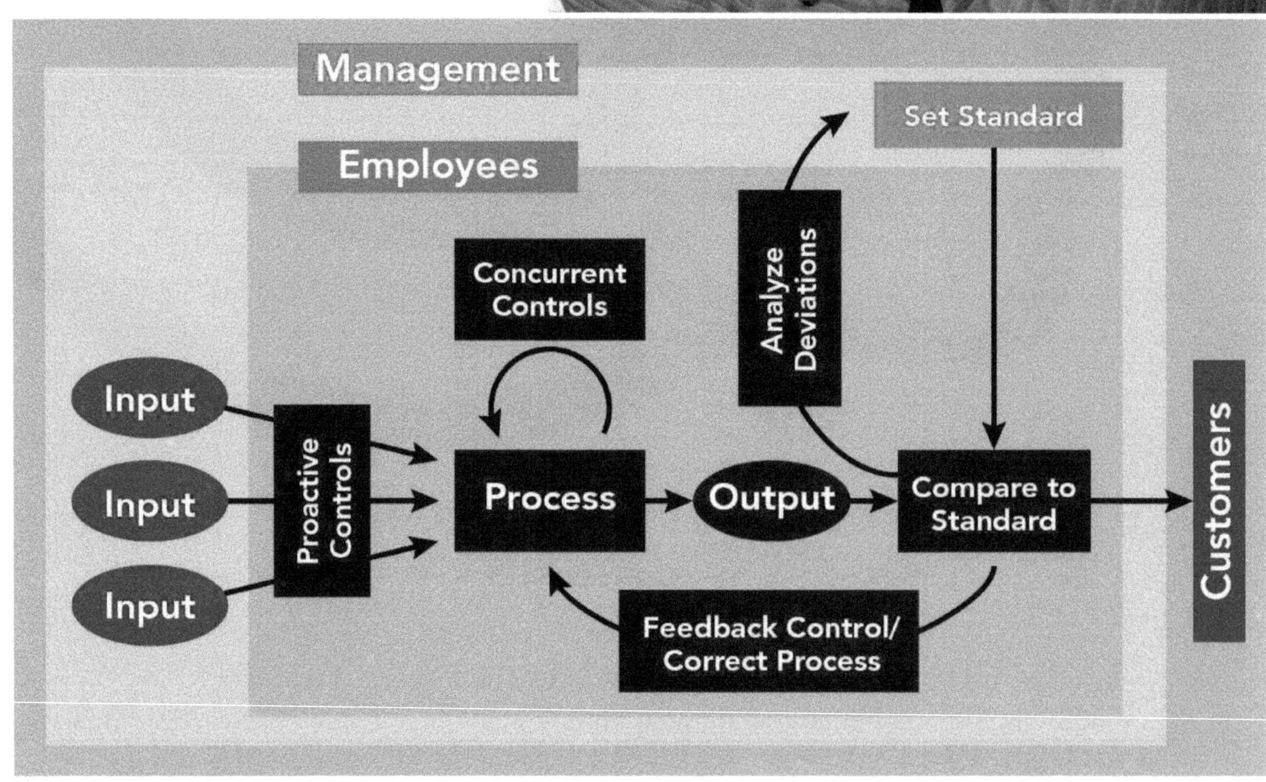

HIMANSHU DEORI

30 WAYS TO KILL DEPRESSION

27.   **Learn to Say No**

Protect your time and energy by setting
boundaries. Saying no to others can mean
saying yes to yourself and your well-being.

HIMANSHU DEORI

30 WAYS TO KILL DEPRESSION

28.   **Develop Self-Compassion**

Treat yourself with the kindness you'd offer a

HIMANSHU DEORI

30 WAYS TO KILL DEPRESSION

friend. Remind yourself that it's okay to struggle and that healing takes time.

HIMANSHU DEORI

30 WAYS TO KILL DEPRESSION

HIMANSHU DEORI

30 WAYS TO KILL DEPRESSION

29. Celebrate Small Wins

Acknowledge and reward every step forward, no matter how small. Recognizing progress builds confidence and reinforces positive habits.

HIMANSHU DEORI

30 WAYS TO KILL DEPRESSION

HIMANSHU DEORI

30 WAYS TO KILL DEPRESSION

30.　**Travel places**

HIMANSHU DEORI

30 WAYS TO KILL DEPRESSION

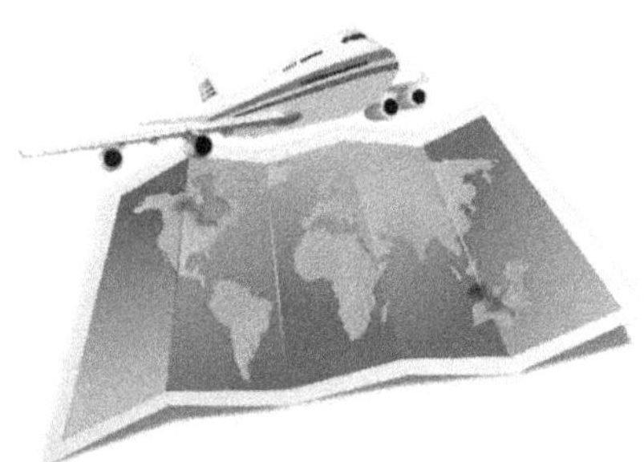

32. THE END

HIMANSHU DEORI

30 WAYS TO KILL DEPRESSION

33. STAY HAPPY AND ENJOY YOUR ONETIME LIFE......

THANK YOU

HIMANSHU DEORI

30 WAYS TO KILL DEPRESSION

THANK YOU FOR READING THIS BOOK

HIMANSHU DEORI

30 WAYS TO KILL DEPRESSION

LET US COME THROUGH SOME OF THE QUOTES ON DEPRESSION.

DOES THE FOLLOWING PICTURES LOOK GOOD?

HIMANSHU DEORI

30 WAYS TO KILL DEPRESSION

HIMANSHU DEORI

30 WAYS TO KILL DEPRESSION

HIMANSHU DEORI

30 WAYS TO KILL DEPRESSION

HIMANSHU DEORI

30 WAYS TO KILL DEPRESSION

OR THE FOLLOWING PICTURES LOOKS GOOD?

HIMANSHU DEORI

30 WAYS TO KILL DEPRESSION

HIMANSHU DEORI

30 WAYS TO KILL DEPRESSION

HIMANSHU DEORI

30 WAYS TO KILL DEPRESSION

HIMANSHU DEORI

30 WAYS TO KILL DEPRESSION

"Our greatest glory is not in never falling, but in rising every time we fall."
— Confucius

This quote reminds us that even in our darkest moments, resilience and the strength to rise again define our true character.

"I didn't want to wake up. I was having a much better time asleep. And that's really sad. It was almost like a reverse nightmare, like when you wake up from a nightmare, you're so relieved. I woke up into a nightmare."
— Ned Vizzini

30 WAYS TO KILL DEPRESSION

Mental pain is less dramatic than physical pain, but it is more common and also harder to bear. The frequent attempt to conceal mental pain increases the burden: It is easier to say 'My tooth is aching' than to say 'My heart is broken.'"
— C.S. Lewis

"You say you're 'depressed' – all I see is resilience. You are allowed to feel messed up and inside out. It doesn't mean you're defective – it just means you're human."
— David Mitchell

 "Even the darkest night will end and the sun will rise."
— Victor Hugo

HIMANSHU DEORI

30 WAYS TO KILL DEPRESSION

"Sometimes it takes an overwhelming breakdown to have an undeniable breakthrough."
— Unknown

"You don't have to control your thoughts. You just have to stop letting them control you."
— Dan Millman

 "There is hope, even when your brain tells you there isn't."
— John Green

HIMANSHU DEORI

30 WAYS TO KILL DEPRESSION

ABOUT THE SERIES OF THE BOOK:

30 ways series:

30 ways series is a series of book that covers topic of self-help and self-improvement especially for the youths.
As the name includes 30 ways, it usually contains 30 summarized points of any topic.

The first book of the series is "30 ways to Kill Depression".

HIMANSHU DEORI

30 WAYS TO KILL DEPRESSION

THANK YOU FOR READING.

HIMANSHU DEORI

30 WAYS TO KILL DEPRESSION

STAY TUNED FOR MORE BOOKS

HIMANSHU DEORI

30 WAYS TO KILL DEPRESSION

JOIN ME AT: www.himanshusblog.free.nf

CONNECT: www.youtube.com/extman

HIMANSHU DEORI

30 WAYS TO KILL DEPRESSION

YOUTUBE QR

HIMANSHU DEORI

30 WAYS TO KILL DEPRESSION

LINKEDIN QR.

HIMANSHU DEORI

30 WAYS TO KILL DEPRESSION

HIMANSHU DEORI

30 WAYS TO KILL DEPRESSION

INSTAGRAM QR

HIMANSHU DEORI

30 WAYS TO KILL DEPRESSION

HIMANSHU DEORI

30 WAYS TO KILL DEPRESSION

HIMANSHU DEORI

30 WAYS TO KILL DEPRESSION

THANK YOU

HIMANSHU DEORI

30 WAYS TO KILL DEPRESSION

HIMANSHU DEORI

30 WAYS TO KILL DEPRESSION

ABOUT THE AUTHOR:

Himanshu Deori is a Young Indian Author from Indian State of Assam. He has written two Fictional Novels previously titled as ' The 245 Days ' published in 2023 and ' Andria 2.0 ' published in 2024. He is currently pursuing his Engineering from Dibrugarh University. He also owns a blogging website www.himanshusblog.free.nf where he posts articles and blogs, and also a YouTube Channel named as ' Ext Man '' where he posts science and Tech Videos. He has won many awards for best poster and paper presentation competitions in his early college life.

HIMANSHU DEORI

30 WAYS TO KILL DEPRESSION

HIMANSHU DEORI

30 WAYS TO KILL DEPRESSION

THANK YOU NOTE:

Dear Reader,

Thank you from the bottom of my heart for picking up 30 Ways to Kill Depression. Your decision to invest in this book is not just a step toward personal growth but also a source of encouragement for me as an author.

Writing this book was a deeply personal journey, and knowing that it has reached you means the world to me. I truly hope that the insights and strategies within these pages help you navigate your path toward healing and happiness.

HIMANSHU DEORI

30 WAYS TO KILL DEPRESSION

Your support, whether through purchasing, reading, or sharing your thoughts, fuels my passion to continue writing and sharing valuable perspectives. If this book has made a difference in your life, I would love to hear from you. Your feedback and stories inspire me more than you know.

Thank you for being a part of this journey. Stay strong, stay hopeful, and remember—you are never alone.

With gratitude,

[Himanshu Deori]
 Author

HIMANSHU DEORI

30 WAYS TO KILL DEPRESSION

ABOUT THE 30 WAYS SERIES:

"The '30 Ways' series is a collection of insightful books that tackle vital issues and topics, summarizing each subject in a concise 30-point guide. For instance, the inaugural volume of the series, '30 Ways to Kill Depression,' was published in 2025

HIMANSHU DEORI

30 WAYS TO KILL DEPRESSION

HIMANSHU DEORI

30 WAYS TO KILL DEPRESSION

HIMANSHU DEORI

HIMANSHU DEORI

30 WAYS TO KILL DEPRESSION

OTHER BOOKS BY THE AUTHOR

'The 245 Days published in 2023'

The 245 Days is a book about a 16-year-old student who studies hard for 245 days to get into his dream college. The book is about the student's life events during his preparation for his 10th board exams.

Buy links:

https://www.amazon.in/245-DAYS-studying-describes-preparation/dp/B0BXNWZ4CV

https://notionpress.com/read/the-245-days?srsltid=AfmBOoqeNDbD5NB7KHVuiaxUuE07Fz7std6mJ-1esppv5kdl-cPdlNxl

https://www.flipkart.com/245-days-16-year-old-average-student-mission-hard-studying-top-his-10-th-boards-describes-everyday-life-events-during-preparation/p/itm0cbb5478f9288?pid=9798890021533&cmpid=product.share.pp&lid=LSTBOK97988900215339CNH9K

HIMANSHU DEORI

30 WAYS TO KILL DEPRESSION

'Andria2.0 published in 2024'

Andria 2.0 is a book by Himanshu Deori about an advanced artificial humanoid robot developed in 2085. The book is available in paperback and as an eBook

Buy links

https://notionpress.com/read/andria-2-0#:~:text=Andria%202.0%20is%20about%20an%20Advanced%20Artificial,who%20passed%20out%20from%20IIT%20Guwahati%20.

https://www.flipkart.com/andria-2-0/p/itme1d3a5bbdc006?pid=9798892770163&lid=LSTBOK9798892770163UJ9SA9&marketplace=FLIPKART&cmpid=content_book_8965229628_gmc

https://www.amazon.in/ANDRIA-2-0-story-Himanshu-Deori-ebook/dp/B0CSFHZFGV#:~:text=ANDRIA%202.0:%20The%20story%20of%20a%20Robot,:%20Deori%2C%20Himanshu%20:%20Amazon.in:%20Kindle%20Store.

HIMANSHU DEORI

www.ingramcontent.com/pod-product-compliance
Lightning Source LLC
Chambersburg PA
CBHW040147110726
48005CB00018B/2675